101 Youth Coaching Tips

LifeTips Book Series

Jim Frey
LifeTips Youth Coaching Expert Guru

Text copyright © 2009 LifeTips. All rights reserved.

LIFETIPS PRESIDENT: Byron White

SERIES EDITOR: Holly Bauer

All rights reserved. No part of this book may be reproduced in any form, by photostat, microfilm, xerography, or any other means, or incorporated into any information retrieval system, electronic or mechanical, without the written permission of the copyright owner.

All inquires should be addressed to:

LifeTips 101 Book Series
77 N. Washington Street
Suite 3B
Boston, MA 02114

http://www.lifetips.com

International Standard Book No. 978-1-60275-049-4

This book is intended for use as an informational guide and entertainment purposes and should not be used as a substitute for any professional medical care or treatment, professional legal advice or professional financial guidance.

Contents

Editor's Note	4
Author's Note	5
Before You Begin	7
You Volunteered. Now What?	17
Practice, Practice, Practice	31
Game On	51
Building a Team	65
Parents	73
Sportsmanship	85
Administrivia	95
Appendix	107

A Note from the Editor

I can't claim to have ever been much of an athlete, although I did give sports a few attempts throughout my young life—I was a gymnast for about three weeks in kindergarten, played softball for a couple of years in elementary (where I learned to play poker in the dugout and made daisy chains in the outfield), and warmed the basketball bench for a year or two in middle school. Needless to say, athletic activity wasn't something I took extremely seriously as a kid.

In retrospect, I was never a member of what Jim Frey refers to in this book as a "play-to-win" team. We were really just there to have fun (at least I was) and get some exercise. While I've never been particularly athletically-inclined and never envisioned myself pursuing athletics seriously, I think that my time playing sports would have been more constructive had there been a better balance of "play-to-win" and "play-for-fun."

In this book, Jim addresses the need for that balance between fun and competition and gives the aspiring (or even seasoned) coach the tools to have a successful season, covering everything from the small, administrative details to how to deal with the ever-vexing teenage personality. This really is an indispensable resource for anybody planning on or thinking about coaching (or assisting) a youth team.

Holly Bauer, editor

A Note from the Author

Coaching is an ongoing journey that I began over twelve years ago when my eldest daughter, Kaitlin, started playing sports at the local YMCA. She played T-ball, and while the coaches did a fantastic job, I found myself thinking things like, "They ought to be teaching the girls this," and "They should be showing them that." My rational self knew that the coaches were doing their very best and that the players were having fun, but (and you knew there had to be a "but") I thought that I might do better. I decided that I could either shut up and cheer or start coaching, so I volunteered the next season to coach T-ball and have been hooked on coaching ever since.

I've only been able to continue coaching for so many years because of the support, encouragement, and love from my wife, Debbie, who has borne the brunt of my frustrations and coaching mistakes and can always be counted on for a smile, a kiss, and a "you'll get 'em next time." Without her, I doubt that I would have lasted two seasons.

Early on, I only coached when my children played for me, so each of them has played for the "old man" at some point. Kaitlin experienced all of my early coaching snafus and ranting and raving, Sarah endured my lack of experience with soccer and subsequent misunderstanding of it, Jenny gladly put up with my volleyball mania, and Jake bore the brunt of my basketball and baseball frustrations. All of my children have been great sports and were always willing to be coached by me—I have a great appreciation for their patience and express my love and thanks to all of them.

Besides my own family, hundreds of other families have entrusted their children to me as a coach. Without their encouragement, feedback, and support, I would not have had as much fun and gotten as much joy as I have.

Jim Frey

Before You Begin

1 | Why You've Become a Coach

To all of you who have decided to share your time and efforts as a coach, I tip my hat and bid you welcome! You are about to embark on a rewarding and challenging journey. Whether the sport you're coaching is one that you are a pro at or one that you have no experience with doesn't matter—the kids will look up to you and think you're a hero.

Most of you are likely very competitive and have a burning desire to win. To keep perspective, try a mantra along the lines of, "I'm here to help the kids, the players should be learning the game and having fun." I would hope that as a coach of youth sports, your goal is to prepare the players to play at the next level, if they so choose. If you're coaching young children (as in, prekindergarten through second grade), then you want to make this first experience one that introduces the sport and makes it fun. Your goals should be to make the players avid participants and to make them want to play more. One of the rewarding side benefits is that years later, you will meet these players as young men and women and they will still call you "Coach." It's a nice feeling. The most positive feedback you can receive comes in the form of the children's desire to keep playing. At their early ages, try to give every player a chance to play each position so that they can learn every aspect of the game. You probably decided to be a coach because you wanted to share your passion and knowledge of the sport. Keep in mind that the game is for the players and not for you to relive those thrilling days of yesteryear. You've had your shot, now give them theirs.

2 | Will Your Child Play for You?

Many people get into coaching because of their own children. Parents want to make sure that their kids have the best experience possible, and some want them to follow in their footsteps. Before you start, consider sitting down and talking with your child. I know that if you ask them if they want you to coach, they will quickly say yes. Duh! It's time with you! Because you have begun to involve them, they will feel good about being asked.

It is difficult, however, for your child to distinguish between the you that is "Mom" or "Dad" and the you that is "Coach." You will have to take the lead on this. Make sure to tell your child that you will always love her, win or lose, and that she will always be your favorite player, even if she misses the winning shot.

During this discussion, you need to share with your child/player what expectations you have for her. How do you want her to practice? Make sure your child knows that she will not be playing every minute of every game and that she will not always be the "star" player. It can be difficult to have these types of conversations with your child, but it is very important that you communicate these thoughts to her. You might need to have this conversation more than once over the course of the season (just because you had the talk once does not mean that your child remembers or even fully understood what you were saying in the first place). It bears repetition. In addition to talking with your child, you have the difficult task of objectively assessing her talent. It's unfair to play your child all the time at the expense of the other players, and creating lineups will ensure that you don't show preference.

3 | Remember: The Game Is for the Kids

When your competitive juices get flowing, it's sometimes difficult to step back and remember that you are coaching for the kids. When your players can't seem to recall how to execute the play that you've just spent the last three practices perfecting, take a deep breath—they're still learning. The thrill of just playing has them so keyed up and enthusiastic that they're lucky to remember which end is up.

It's likely that, at some point, you will have labored over developing a play that you feel is a sure fire way to score points. After patiently teaching your team the ins, outs, and nuances of your masterpiece, you are just dumbfounded when they can't remember how the play works, or even who's supposed to start things off. Okay, it's time to count to ten. Remember: you are the coach and you probably have hours and hours of practice time. This is not some conspiracy to annoy you. Your team has been exposed to your brain child for what, a couple of hours? Maybe three practices? The beauty of being a coach is that, after carefully nurturing and guiding the players along, you will eventually see them suddenly get it, and the play will be executed just like you've seen it a hundred times in your mind.

→

4 | Remember: You're a Parent First, Then a Coach

As you go through your coaching odyssey, you might find yourself gravitating toward a specific sport. It's very important to achieve a balance between being a coach and a parent.

I had to learn this lesson the hard way when my daughter called me out for only ever talking to her about volleyball. I stopped and took a hard look at myself. What happened was, the more that I coached volleyball, the more I became consumed with it. I became a real geek and started surfing the web, reading books, attending classes, and talking, talking, talking volleyball. It got to a point where I was ignoring the rest of what was going on with my children.

So what's the tip here? Yes, it's a little obvious at this point, but make sure to remind yourself once in a while that family comes first. Even though you're having the time of your life coaching, athletics is only a part (a very small part) of what your children's lives are all about. If you find yourself constantly talking about the sport, step back and take a deep breath—your children will be leaving the house sooner than you expect. Enjoy all of their moments, not just the ones that happen on the athletic field.

5 | You Don't Have to Have all the Answers

Few of us youth coaches have the luxury of having graduated with a degree in sports management or having been a professional coach. In most cases, we have full-time jobs and are trying to raise families of our own. We volunteer to coach and then we put pressure on ourselves, thinking that we need to be an encyclopedia of all there is to know about the sport. Don't fall into the ego trap of, "I'm the coach and I am *the* source of all knowledge!"

There are many sources of information at your disposal. No one expects you to be Pat Summit, Bill Parcels, or Joe Torre. Even if you're extremely knowledgeable about your sport, you will find that the players and parents are going to ask questions that you've never even thought about. It's okay to say, "I hadn't thought about that," or "I need to get back to you." What's important is to have an open mind, a willingness to accept suggestions, and a desire to learn more.

While you can't be expected to know everything, there is some information that you MUST know and share in a timely fashion. Local rules, game and practice schedules, and directions to playing venues are all things that players and families need to know, so make sure that you share this information as soon as you can.

6 | Don't Be Afraid to Ask for Help

Once you accept the fact that you don't have to be the sole source of knowledge, you should take the next step and be willing to ask for help. We hesitate to ask for help and volunteers because we all know that everyone is busy with jobs, family, maybe church, and the community just like we are. Don't get caught in the death spiral of thinking that, because you volunteered to be the coach, you MUST do everything yourself! This mistake will cause you undue stress and additional work, and that's certainly not why you became a coach.

Ask the parents if they are interested in helping you coach. Ask for a team parent to help with gathering contact information and communicating with all of the families. There is quite a bit of administrative work that needs to be done to make the team run smoothly. From the sports side of things, solicit favorite practice drills, play formations, and tactics from the families. This will help you to begin building a notebook on coaching.

You will be amazed at how willing people are to help get things going and set up for the season, but also keep in mind that there will be times when you ask for help and hear nothing back. Some families might not have any experience with your sport and have nothing to offer. Others might be reluctant because they haven't played in a long time, and some people might feel uncomfortable advising the coach. Don't despair—at least you've opened the line of communication. Keep at it.

7 | Read a "Dummies" Guide

Part of seeking help might be doing some reading and research on coaching your sport. (The fact that you are reading this is a great first step.) If you've never coached the sport before, the *For Dummies* series is an excellent source of information. These types of books will give you a great start at preparing for practice and understanding the fundamentals of the sport. They will also keep you a step or two in front of the players!

Whether you're a first-time coach or an old pro, the internet is filled with a tremendous amount of coaching information. Search the web for coaching hints and tips and take advantage of practice drills and plays. Whatever your preference, take time to research and read. They say that copying someone or something is the sincerest form of flattery. If you like a drill or a play that another coach has written about, why reinvent the wheel? Coaches love to share their thoughts and ideas. This will make your job a lot easier.

8 | Some Things to Purchase

To make life a bit simpler for you, there are a few things that you should consider purchasing prior to the start of practice:

- A new pair of sport shoes would probably be a good idea, and if you're coaching in a gymnasium, lead by example and change into your game shoes at the gym.

- You could also use a good whistle. This will help a great deal when you're trying to get everyone's attention and stop play quickly. You can find these at any of your local sports stores.
- The next thing you want to consider is a clipboard. This will enable you to keep your practice notes, roster, and lineups in one place. Sporting goods stores sell clipboards that are like classroom white boards, allowing you to use them for drawing up plays during a game.
- The next items to consider purchasing are a hand air pump and pressure gauge. These are handy to have in your bag and you will find that, many times, the practice balls that you use are not inflated to recommended pressure. If you do purchase the pump and gauge, make sure that you also purchase extra needles, as they tend to break very easily.

- You might also consider a folder with multiple sleeves. This will help you with all of the paperwork that you will need to carry.
- Finally, a sports bag to carry all of this equipment around in will help you look smart and look the part.

9 | Plan out the Season

It is almost time to start. The best way to ensure a successful, smooth, and fun-filled season is to sit down and plan things out. You don't need to spend hours and hours planning out every single minute, but a general outline of things that you need or want to accomplish will help you get the most out of your practices. Here are some initial questions to consider:

- Will you hold tryouts or a "player skills assessment" session?
- If you plan on holding tryouts, what sort of skills and abilities are you looking for? Is height or weight a factor?
- Will your team have inexperienced players?
- Do you need to start with the very basics and fundamentals of the sport to develop your players?

The questions could continue, but you get the idea. Once you're able to answer these questions, you'll be better prepared for the practice sessions. Take the time to put your thoughts on paper so that you can refer to them during tryouts.

After you have selected or are given a team, the preseason is a good time to focus on the fundamentals: how to make a left-hand layup, the position to field a ground ball, how to dribble a soccer ball, etc. The preseason is the time during which you can begin to form your team. Also, make sure to allow time for conditioning. Even with young athletes, conditioning is an important part of practice. It lets your players know that there is more to the sport than just going out and playing the game—it takes hard work!

As your competitive season begins, replace some of the fundamental and conditioning drills with tactics and strategy drills, but keep stressing the fundamentals—having a strong platform and knowing how to properly execute a skill will serve your players long after the season ends. By midseason, focus on perfecting your team's offensive and defensive tactics. Ensuring that every player knows where she needs to be during play will set your team apart. As your season begins to wind down, the practices should be filled with more game-like situations. At this point in the season, conditioning should make up just a small percentage (10–15 %) of your practice time.

You Volunteered. Now What?

10 | Tryouts

How will your team be formed? Are you just given a list of players and their contact phone numbers? Will there be a group skills assessment where all the players and all the coaches in the league get together to assess the players' skills and abilities? Each league that you coach in may be different.

You might want to inquire with the league office as to how the players are assigned to teams, just so that you'll be prepared. Talk with the league coordinator or director and ask for any documentation used for the tryouts. You should also take a few minutes to sit and sketch out what your expectations are for the players. Think about trade-offs that you would be willing to make regarding players. Is height or weight important? What game skills do you value most? Prioritize these skills. What will you do when you see a potential player who has some of the best skills, but who also displays a bad attitude or poor sportsmanship?

If you are responsible for the tryout, prepare a set of drills that will allow the players plenty of time to demonstrate their individual skills as well as their team skills. Allow sufficient time for each drill so that you are able to see each athlete several times. Remember to set realistic expectations. Tryouts can be stressful for young athletes, so encourage everyone and try to make it fun.

11 | Document Your Thoughts and Impressions of Each Player

Making notes on your players will help you when talking with your players and parents. For school teams at any level, tryouts can be a major source of anxiety for both you and the players. If you don't know many of the players who are trying out or their names, a good way to learn their names is to write them on two-inch pieces of tan masking tape and have each player stick the name tag on his front left shoulder. Taking the time to write each name and look at each athlete will help you remember later on.

Taking notes during tryouts can be of great assistance when you have to select your team. Prepare an assessment sheet with enough room down the left side to accommodate the name of each player who is trying out. Create columns for the skills that you are looking for in your athletes. Settle on a rating system (A, B, C; 5, 4, 3, 2, 1; or good, better, best) for each skill you'll be assessing. The last column should be a comments area for noting your impressions regarding enthusiasm, athleticism, ability to be a team player, etc. If physical attributes are important, make sure that you take the time to measure and weigh each player and write the information down. At the end of each day's tryout, take time to sit down and review your assessment notes. This will help cement each player's face, name, and abilities.

If you have more than one day of tryouts, have an assessment sheet for each day. The night that you are selecting your team, review each day's tryout sheet (you may want to consolidate everything onto one sheet). Save all the sheets, as you can use your notes later when you give the players feedback.

12 | Selecting Your Team

Your tryouts were a success—you had a record number of athletes show up and things are looking great! Now it's time to select the team. The notes that you made on each player's skills during tryouts will become an invaluable reference tool.

As you consider the makeup of your team, you might want to consider the following: Will you have multiple players for each position? Do you want players to play all the positions or will you ask certain players to specialize at positions? Will good athletes be able to learn the sport or do you want the experienced players? Review your notes and rank the players according to your criteria. Set a goal of having all of the players ranked and then make your selections.

Choosing the first four to seven players is usually easy, as these players have the skills and experience you expect. It's selecting players eight through n that's more difficult. Your notes will help you make the best selections. Use any positive comments you have listed for the players as tie-breakers when everything else is equal.

13 | Call Everyone

If you're coaching at the high school level, you can skip this tip, as most high schools just post the list of players who have made the team. For those of you who have to select a team and contact the players, get in touch with *every* player who tried out for the team. All of the players put themselves on the line and tried their best to make the team—you owe them the courtesy of a phone call, whether they made the team or not.

Before you call, prepare what you want to say to each player. Review your assessment sheets and have something positive to say to each individual. Call and ask for the player directly, and DO NOT leave a phone message. If they're not at home, ask that they call you back. For those whom you've selected, tell them how excited you are and "offer" them a position on the team. Perhaps they've had a change of heart and decided to not play or maybe they want to try another sport. Give them the *option* to say yes.

Congratulate those who accept and give some feedback as to why you chose them. Commend those who didn't make the team for their efforts by telling them that you admire their courage in trying out and by encouraging them to keep working on their skills. Give them an area or two on which they could concentrate to improve.

After you've talked to each athlete, ask to speak with a parent or guardian. Tell the parents exactly what you told the athlete. This will avoid any confusion or miscommunication. Your assessment sheet will prove to be of great value in these discussions, as you can refer to it when parents ask why their child did not make the team. Avoid making comparisons to other athletes when talking with parents; instead, focus on the ways in which their child could improve.

14 | How Many on the Team?

As you consider the makeup of your team, you need to decide how many team members you want on it. Need versus want is a decision that only you can make. You'll need to have enough players to fill all of the positions with adequate substitutions. Don't forget to account for the times at which you won't have a full team due to illness, family vacations, and emergencies—you don't want to have to forfeit a game because you don't have enough players.

Your being the only coach can also have an effect on how many players you keep. With a larger number of players, being the only coach can limit the time that you can devote to each individual player. For sports such as basketball, volleyball, and baseball, it's not a bad idea to have an even number of players; with an even number, you can pair up the players for drills, skills development, and warm-ups. This will leave you free to move around, observe the players, and provide feedback and encouragement instead of warming up players. When deciding on the number of players, decide if you want to hold scrimmages. You'll need enough to have two teams; otherwise you'll have to recruit parents to fill the open positions.

15 | First Team Meeting

At this point, it might seem like you've been doing everything *but* coaching. You're just itching to get onto the playing field and take your team through their paces. Taking the time now to organize things, communicate with parents, share ideas, and set up schedules will make your coaching time so much more meaningful and fun.

It's important to plan out what you want to say to your players and their parents. The first team meeting does not have to be long—thirty to forty minutes should be sufficient. For the younger players (kindergarten through fifth grade), you might be able to have the meeting right after the first practice. There is important information that needs to be exchanged at this meeting (have I mentioned that this meeting is important?). If you have not done so, get everyone's email address, as email will be the fastest way of distributing information. At this point, you will have the schedule of the games and practices for the team. Be ready to hand this out or send it in an email. Prepare a short, two to three-minute biography about yourself and tell everyone where the practices and the games will be held. If you have a younger team, snacks can sometimes be the highlight of the game. Do you want snacks? If so, what kind of snacks? Are there any food allergies to be aware of? And what about uniforms? When will they be available? You need to find this information and communicate it to the families.

16 | Set Goals and Expectations

When you first meet the team, you will want to share your goals and expectations with everyone. It is very important that everyone hears this, and you should also repeat this information several times over the course of the season—don't assume that because you shared your goals and expectations once that everyone agrees or has the same understanding. There are many items that you need to consider and share with everyone, such as:

- When do you want the players to show up for practice? Five minutes before, fifteen minutes before, or right when practice is scheduled?
- How early do you want players to show up for games?
- Is practice attendance a requisite in order to play?
- Do you stress fundamentals?
- Offensive and defensive strategies, if age appropriate
- What the players can expect to learn (this is important for both the players and parents)

17 | For the Players

This tip should save you some frustration and aggravation. Players *and* parents need to know early on what your expectations are regarding practice. Do you want them dressed out and ready to go when practice starts? Even with the younger players, you should have the discussion that getting to practice when coach wants them there is their responsibility, not their parents'. Do you encourage your players to do more than just come to practice? Heaven forbid that players practice foul shots, service tosses, or run a few extra laps for conditioning outside of practice!

Set your expectations early about good sportsmanship and what the consequences are for poor sportsmanship. If you agree with the following, talk to the players about "Practicing like they want to play in a game!" Because of today's professional sports, where players often do not feel like they need to be role models and practice appears unnecessary, young athletes often get the mistaken idea that all they have to do is show up on game day and everything will be fine. If the players don't learn to play as a team with solid fundamentals in practice, then how are they going to perform in a competitive game? Sloppy practice habits lead to sloppy game play.

18 | Have a Package Prepared to Distribute to Each Family

We've covered many items that should be discussed during this first meeting with the players and parents. To ensure that the information stays in long-term memory, a handout is a good idea. The handout should contain the schedule of practices and games (with locations), email addresses of the parents, game rules and any location-specific rule changes or amendments, and your short biography.

For the younger players, snacks are an important item. If you're planning on allowing snacks after games, you might want to have a discussion in the handout about allowable snacks. You might offer your recommendations: Power Bars, water, Gatorade/Powerade, etc. Snacks are not mandatory, but you should have the discussion at this meeting. For the outdoor sports that might be played in hot weather (for example, soccer), keeping the players hydrated can be a concern. During breaks and halftime, plenty of water should be on hand for the players. If it's really hot and muggy, having cold, wet wash cloths is a great way to help keep the players cooled down.

19 | Competitive Philosophy

Something that really should (dare I say "must"?) be discussed is your personal philosophy about or approach to competition. Do you play to play, and play to win? Will all of the players get playing time? Do you have a different lineup for each game, or will you put the strongest players into the same positions? Will only the best players play unless the game is out of hand? Will all players play for the same amount of time? This is, at times, a sensitive subject for players and parents. If you address the point early and remind players and parents throughout the season of your approach, then your dealings with them will be easier.

Once you've chosen a competitive approach, make sure that you stick with it. It seems like such a small item, but this can cause a lot of team heartache, hurt feelings, and angry parents. It's difficult, if not impossible, to play to win and get all of the players equal amounts of playing time. How you deal with playing time can also be affected by your competitive approach. Do you coach in order to prepare the players to play at the next level? Is your approach to build the players' fundamental capabilities? Are you showcasing some individual players to play in a more advanced league? As you answer these questions, you will begin to formulate your competitive philosophy, which will assist you in communicating with players and parents.

20 | Playing Time

If this is just a "fun" recreation league, then playing all of the players for equal amounts of time is a great approach. Some leagues even have rules that all players have to play for specified amounts of time (for example, one quarter in basketball, three innings in baseball, and one half of play in soccer).

If the league you're competing in does not have rules governing playing time, here are some things to consider: Create a lineup that has a combination of skilled and less-skilled players and encourage the better players to help the less-skilled players. This mixing of players helps to avoid having all of your weaker ones on the field at the same time, and your team will play more consistently and will likely be more successful throughout the game. Early in the season, try different lineups, mixing and matching different players.

For the younger ages (prekindergarten through fifth grade), try to give all of the players an opportunity to play every position. There will be players who have phobias about playing particular positions because of fear of failure. Work with them in practice to show them that they can play those positions. Encourage them to try their best and cheer them on when they succeed. By the end of the season, you want all of your players to feel like they've made a contribution and have learned about all of the positions played.

21 | Timeliness

When you're coaching teams that play after school, getting to practice and games on time can be a challenge. You need to stress the importance of timeliness to your team. Define your expectations and hold the players accountable. Your practice time is usually limited, so if players are not ready to begin practice on time, you will not be able to maximize the time given and will have difficulty keeping your practices running smoothly.

Even worse is having your players show up to games right when they're supposed to start or a few minutes late. Not knowing which players are available to play will make your job exasperating! Juggling a lineup during a game can become a distraction. Emphasize to your players that they need to be on time and ready to practice or play early. Specifically define how many minutes before the game you want the players on the court or field.

When practice begins, players need to be fully dressed for the sport, rather than sitting on the sidelines and lacing up shoes or putting on pads. You might find that younger players tend to want to sit and chat, even if they've just spent the last eight hours in school together. That's okay, but not to the detriment of the practice or game. Tell the players to come to the venue ready to begin at the specified time. Being early allows players time to dress, talk, and prepare mentally.

22 | Food and Snacks

Something to consider is whether or not you want to have snacks brought to the practices and games. If you're coaching in a recreation league for younger players, one of the highlights of game day is often the after-game snack. Is this something you want to do? Snacks for both games and practices can become rather expensive. If you're coaching a school team, do you want the team to have a pre-game snack? If you decide to have snacks, you might want to consider some guidelines. You also need to ask if any of your players have food allergies—you don't want anyone breaking out in hives (or worse) because you didn't ask. Sports drinks or water, Power Bars, chips, cookies, or cereal bars are healthy options. Try to avoid soda, candy, doughnuts, and caffeinated drinks. For the pre-game snack, fruit (grapes are always a hit), cereal bars, Power Bars, bagels, and cheese and crackers are all healthy and supply needed energy.

Regardless of whether or not you have snacks, make sure that all of the players come to practice and games with water. It is extremely important that everyone (even you, Coach) stays hydrated. Allow times during practice for the players to get drinks of water. To ensure that practice doesn't digress and valuable time doesn't get lost, give the players ninety seconds to get a drink. If anyone returns after that time, have the entire team face a consequence, such as crunches, sprints, or push-ups (this helps tremendously with timeliness).

23 | Will You Have Captains?

This tip is more applicable to school teams, but recreation leagues sometimes also have team captains.

For the rec leagues, you might have a different player act as captain at each game. This gives everyone a chance to "call the flip" and meet the officials. For school teams, having captains is a bit more formal, but not absolutely required. You could choose to rotate through the team as discussed previously, or you can formalize the positions. If you choose to have formal captains, I would suggest that you have two. One captain can be elected by the team and the other appointed by you. For middle school teams, the selection of captains is usually a popularity contest, which means that the best player for the position doesn't always get chosen—this is why *you* appoint a captain as well.

When you have the discussion about choosing a captain with your players, talk to them about what you expect from the captain. Who do the players want to lead them?

Practice, Practice, Practice

24 | First Practice

Now we're getting somewhere! It's your first practice and you're wondering how you will ever fill up the time allotted. If you don't take ten or fifteen minutes prior to practice to lay out what you want to accomplish, you'll find yourself asking that very question quite frequently. By coming to practice ready to start, you'll lead by example. Bring your clipboard with your practice objectives, your whistle, and your hand air pump, and you've made a good start. Two additional things that you might want to bring are a black or dark-colored marker and masking tape.

As the players show up, greet them, introduce yourself, and ask each player what name she likes to be called. Write the names down on the masking tape, tear the strips off, and have the players put them on their chests. This will help you learn the names of your players and will give the other players a chance to learn their teammates' names. You might start this first practice by having each player give her name, grade, and how long she's been playing this sport.

The first practice is also a great time to remind the players that you want them to practice like they want to play in the game. You don't have to be serious and totally focused during every second of practice, but you want the players to focus and concentrate during certain parts. Make sure to tell them when you need them to bear down and focus. If you have not yet had a parent meeting, you can take a few minutes at the end of practice to pass out the schedule, email addresses, etc., to the parents.

25 | First Aid

If you're using a facility such as a YMCA for practice and games, you can skip to the next tip, because the Y has personnel on-site who are trained in first aid and a first aid kit is always available. High schools and middle schools usually have a first aid kit somewhere in the building (I emphasize "somewhere"—the secret will be finding the one person who knows where that location is in the school). Find out where the first aid kit is located and what you have to do to gain access to it. I admit that I really don't know too much about first aid beyond what I've learned first-hand from being the injured athlete. Hopefully, in your coaching career, you will never have to deal with a serious injury. At least be prepared for the normal bumps and bruises. It's a good idea to know where the kit is or to build one for your own use. Borrowing from the Boy Scouts of America, "Be prepared"! For your kit, you need not spend a fortune. There are a few very simple items that you can have at practices and games that will help you handle the minor cuts and scrapes that you may encounter:

- Instant cold pack (or a bag of ice)
- Bandages (sheer and flexible)
- Disposable gloves
- First aid tape
- Antiseptic wipes
- First aid cream
- Scissors

There are a number of excellent sites you can visit on the internet that will help refresh your memory on how to handle sprained ankles and minor cuts and bruises. Here are a couple of examples: exrx.net/ExInfo/FirstAid.html or firstaid.about.com/od/breaksandsprains/qt/06_sports.html. If you really want to learn more, there are many books and pamphlets that you can purchase.

26 | Practice Like You Want to Play in the Game

Almost every player that I have coached has wanted to play the game or at least scrimmage far more than she's wanted to practice. Practice is boring. With running, doing suicides, or conditioning, the players will find a hundred reasons why they don't want to practice. With today's professional athletes often saying that they don't need to practice, is it surprising that young athletes think the same thing? Impress on the players that it is extremely difficult, if not impossible, to show up and play like Tom Brady or LeBron James or Derek Jeter.

Another point about practice is learning what your teammates can and cannot do. Knowing what you can expect from them, where they will be on the field/court, and how they will react are all very important to learning how to play as a team. When players focus and concentrate at practice and learn to run plays and improve their skill levels, this all ultimately translates into a successful group of players who play as a team. Youth players are just beginning to learn the sport, regardless of what they will tell you, so they have not conditioned their minds or bodies to perform at peak levels. Even when adult athletes don't practice hard, it is difficult at game time to turn the competitive switch to "full speed" and maintain that for an extended period of time. Practice is what creates and develops this ability.

Another way to prepare for the game is to practice the fundamentals at home: foul shots, ball handling, dribbling, and serving are all necessities, but are not usually given much practice time. Encourage your players to practice at home. You might even give them some drills that they can practice at home with a sibling or a parent. Who has taken your advice and done some work outside of practice will be very evident.

27 | Do Versus Don't

If I say, "Don't think of a pink elephant," what is the first thing that pops into your head? A pink elephant, of course! Tell your players how you want them to do things. When they're practicing a skill and not doing it quite right, tell them what they are doing that is correct, and then tell them what they can focus on to improve. It's about telling them what *to* do, rather than what *not* to do. Yes, this is all a matter of semantics, but every coaching book that I have read and the coaches that I have had an opportunity to observe have all stressed this same simple concept. For young athletes, it appears that when you say something like, "Don't bend at the waist," the word "don't" is somehow filtered out and what their brains hear is, "Bend at the waist!" You want to get your players to envision the best and correct way of doing things, so why not coach them that way?

The idea here is to decide how you want to coach your players and how you will talk to them. This may be one of the most difficult things to do (at least it has been for me). I even play a game with my players by challenging them to catch me saying "don't" instead of "do." I tell them that every time they catch me using the word "don't," I'll drop immediately and do five push-ups. This also guarantees that they listen more closely to what I'm saying. You will also find yourself searching for a positive way of explaining what you expect or want them to accomplish. It's difficult, but it's a much stronger and effective way to coach.

28 | Keep Control of the Practice

The practice time that the team has is at a premium and usually too short, and you have a lot of things to share with the players. A difficult skill to master is keeping control of your practice without becoming a tyrant or a dictator. To keep players' attention, you might suggest to them that, if their lips are moving, they cannot possibly be listening to what you're saying. Also effective is to stop talking and stare at the offending players; fairly quickly, the conversation(s) stop and you'll get their attention. You can also set consequences for interrupting, such as running laps or sprints, to get your point across.

During the school year, sitting at school for seven or eight hours a day gives the players an incredible amount of extra energy that they desperately need to expend; the last thing that they want to do is be still and attentive. You can help burn off some of this energy by opening practice with some fast-paced warm-ups. Get the players moving. They could work on running the bases, playing 3-on-3, doing a three-person weave—anything to get them involved and take the edge off of their pent-up energy. This will get the players focused and help them to concentrate on what you say during practice. After you run a drill or scrimmage and want to bring the players into a huddle to discuss something, a good idea is to have all of the balls placed on the ground, between the players' feet. There is an almost compulsive need to dribble, bounce, kick, pass, or spin a ball when players are gathered to "listen" to the coach, and placing the ball between their feet eliminates this potential distraction.

29 | Learn all of the Players' Names

Have you ever worked with someone who goes to introduce you and doesn't know your name, or have someone constantly call you by the wrong name? How did you feel? What was your opinion of that person? Now put yourself in a player's shoes and imagine how she will feel if you can't remember her name.

As mentioned previously, you can write the players' names on pieces of masking tape and have them wear them as name tags. If your sport involves a hat, then you could have each player write her name on the underside bill of the cap (this has the added benefit of identifying hats left after games or practices). Another method is to take a picture of each player and note the name on each one. You might have to say each name out loud several times during the first few practices to really cement them in your long-term memory.

By learning the players' names, you will be putting a face with a name and showing the players that you take a real interest in them. Also, everyone likes to be called by her preferred name. Learning everyone's name will also allow you to more accurately capture your thoughts about each player's capabilities and attitudes.

30 | Come to Practice Prepared

One of the best ways to ensure that your practices are fun, productive, and less stressful for you is to take the time prior to practice to plan out what you want to accomplish. This planning should only take ten or fifteen minutes and you can break your practice time down into ten to fifteen-minute increments. Breaking up practices like this keeps things flowing, keeps the players engaged, and will allow you to get a sense of what the players need to work on.

Set aside a few minutes at the start of practice for the team to warm up. You can structure warm-ups with jogging laps, stretching, and some conditioning, or you may choose to have a game. For instance, in volleyball, you can have two games of 3-on-3 using only a ten-by-fifteen court area on each side of the net. Whichever method you choose, get the players loosened up and thinking about the sport. As mentioned previously, you can change the emphasis of the practices as you progress through the season. Allow for water breaks, and ensure that all of the players stay hydrated.

Every team that I've coached always wants to scrimmage. Use their desire to scrimmage as an incentive: "If you do the drills well and listen, then we *might* scrimmage at the end of practice." Too many times, scrimmages are used as a time-filler until the end of practice. Always stay involved, both for safety reasons and to reinforce what you want. When you scrimmage, have an objective in mind of what you want the team to execute and accomplish. If you've been practicing basketball screens, then make the players set at least two screens before a shot is taken. If you've been practicing outlet passes up the sides for soccer, then make them do that before advancing for a shot on the goal. Use the scrimmage as a controlled way of perfecting what they've learned. At the very end of the scrimmage (the last two or three minutes), you might reward them by allowing them to just scrimmage.

31 | Keep all of the Players Involved

As you plan your practice activities, do so with the goal of keeping all of your players involved. The quickest way to lose their attention is to have them standing around, not engaged in the practice. If the players stand for more than sixty seconds, their focus will wander and they'll want to goof around, distract other players, and will quickly forget why and what you want them to do. If one of your objectives for a practice is to work with just a subset of the players, that's okay as long as you have a concurrent activity for the other players to work on. Players can always work to improve fundamentals. Assign them a drill to execute while you concentrate on the other players. Whenever possible, break down the drills so that everyone stays involved and busy (shagging balls, handing balls to you, executing the drill, etc.). The key is to keep everyone alert and involved.

Keeping the activities short helps the players stay focused. Some of this timing has to come as a result of trial and error. You want the activity to be long enough that each player has the opportunity to get several touches with the ball, as this will allow them to be successful and improve. Keep your drills fast-paced. Players completing a drill should be running back to the end of the line—they should be in constant motion. If they're caught walking, make them run a lap or do some crunches or push-ups. This is good conditioning.

32 | Play Games (Make the Drills "Game-Like")

One of the first teams that I coached was a second and third grade girls' soccer team. We practiced skills development and did drills at every practice. At the end of each practice, I would think, "They've got it!" and I'd be excited to see them execute at the next game. When that next game came along, however, it was like they had never practiced and didn't have a clue what to do. Huh? What's going on here? The players were not able to easily translate the drills from practice into team play in the game. So what can you do to help your players?

As you plan your practices, make your drills "game-like" and have your players execute the skills in a game situation. Here's an example for volleyball: Strong, consistent, overhand service is very important in volleyball. Rather than having your players stand at the base lines and serve twenty or twenty-five balls (what server ever serves that many times in a row anyway?), divide your team in half and place each new team on either end of the court. The goal is to be the first team to 25. Tell them that the score is tied 18-to-18 or 20-to-20 (pick a score). One side will begin serving, one player after another, each serving once. As long as the service is in play, their score is increased. If they miss a service, the other team begins serving and serves until they miss or until they reach 25. This is a fun way to practice, as it adds a game-like atmosphere to the drill, gets the players familiar with game pressure, and prepares them to execute in a game. You can even spice things up with a consequence for the team that loses or a reward for the winning group.

33 | Practices

Have you ever played for a coach who was so predictable that you knew exactly what was going to happen at every practice, every time? How much fun were those practices? As your season progresses, the players will need to concentrate on different skills. Early on, the fundamentals are important skills to master, and conditioning will be more important during the early-to-midseason than it will be later in the season. You get the drift. Toward the end of the season, the fundamental drills should occupy just a brief portion of practice time. As the season progresses, take the time to modify your practice regime to meet your team's needs.

After each game, you may want to take a few minutes to review how your team played. What went well and what could use more work? You can use this input to build practice schedules.

34 | Fun Practice Activities

Everyone has heard the adage, "All work and no play makes Jack a dull boy." Since you're asking your players to practice like they want to play during the game, they will be expending extra physical and mental effort in practice. To expect this for the entire time is unrealistic. To give your players a break and let them recharge, plan some games or fun activities during the practice. You don't need to dedicate a lot of time to this, but you'll see the benefits of having a break in the practice and having a little fun.

"I don't know any fun activities" is a common reaction from reluctant coaches. There are loads of suggestions out on the web, so do a little searching on your own. Here are some things you might consider: Early in the season, try doing some team-building activities during practice. Here's a modified "blind man's bluff": set up an obstacle course on the field, blindfold two or three players, and have the rest of the players issue instructions/commands for the players navigating the course. You can time this and reward the best times. Maybe keep a bag of miniature candy bars and reward the entire team if they perform a drill the way you want them to. You can also do a progressive tag game. By taking just a small amount of time away from practice and doing an activity, your players will stay fresh and focused.

35 | In Youth Sports, Fundamentals Should Come First

Have you ever attended a game in which few, if any, of the players demonstrated good, solid fundamentals? It's been a personal gripe of mine for years to see ten, eleven, and twelve-year-olds playing baseball and not knowing how to cleanly field a ground ball, judge a fly ball, or hold the bat correctly. Or what about basketball players who have no idea how to set picks, bounce pass, or effectively box out the opponent for a rebound? Unfortunately, this is sometimes the case for higher-level teams, even into the college ranks. There's just not enough emphasis on solid fundamental development. As you coach, you'll encounter teams that just hammer the competition. Some teams will simply be comprised of better athletes; however, when two equally-matched teams face each other, the one with stronger fundamentals almost always wins.

The great thing about teaching fundamentals is that players can practice them at home or during recess. As your players master these skills, your team will become better and win more games. More importantly, you'll enable your players to continue onto higher levels of play. As players get into high school athletics, coaches look for players who demonstrate a strong grasp of fundamentals during tryout scrimmages. After all, JV and Varsity coaches don't have time to teach the basics; the players either have them or they don't, and at that point, it's too late to teach them.

36 | When Your Players Get the Heebie-Jeebies

I don't know if I spelled the words right, but I can almost guarantee that during some practices, you will notice that the players are easily distracted or unable to listen to what you're saying. I call this the heebie-jeebies. This is usually more prevalent during the school year, when they've patiently sat through long days of study without running, playing, and having fun, and now here's a coach trying to make them bear down and concentrate more!

When younger players become distracted, it's a good idea to blow your whistle, stop practice, and have them run laps. Have them run at least two, and while they're running additional laps, tell them to sit down in a circle near you when they get tired. This quick activity takes the edge off of their pent-up energy, and when they come to the circle, you'll find them much more pleasant and manageable. For older, more experienced teams, start practice with a high-energy drill or game to get them expending some energy. If necessary during practice, call a timeout and have the team get into a huddle. Remind them of what you expect and assure them that you know that there's a perfect skill execution hiding in them. They usually get the point, and it's also good for players to experience timeouts and get used to forming a huddle.

37 | Drills Only Go so Far

Earlier, we discussed the reality that players sometimes have trouble translating the skills that they develop in drills over to games.

Drills are valuable and necessary for teaching strong fundamentals and maneuvers in a sport. Players, once they believe they've mastered a given maneuver, will stop concentrating and won't practice like they want to play in the game. To keep your players focused on perfecting their skills, try making practice drills competitive. For instance, can a group of players make twenty foul shots in two minutes? Or, can a group be first to successfully navigate a cone course using only one-touch passes? You can reward the best or first finishers with candy or gum, or you could set consequences such as crunches, sprints, or push-ups for the slower finishers. If you don't want to use food as a reward, call the team together and recognize the group that achieved the goal and give them a quick cheer. From a team perspective, you might challenge the players to complete a series of skills, such as ten good passes, sets, and spikes for volleyball.

By adding a little competition and pressure to your drills, you encourage the players to concentrate on what they're doing and you allow them to develop a routine. The players will also get used to depending on their teammates in order to be successful. You will find that your practices are livelier and faster-paced when the players are engaged and concentrating.

38 | When Your Practice Plan Just Isn't Working

You've taken the time to develop practice plans, you're getting fairly adept at maximizing the available practice time, and things are moving along nicely when suddenly, you run into a brick wall! There's no passion in the practice, the players are listless and disinterested—your practice has a "flat tire." First of all, don't blame the players—they have not formed a conspiracy to aggravate you and fray your last nerve. Take a deep breath, call a quick water break, and take a look at what you have planned. A reset may be in order.

Try a five or ten-minute scrimmage. Set parameters for the scrimmage, such as only shooting from the left side, or only hitting to right field, or only using three dribbles. Once the players have started to focus, you can extend the scrimmage a bit longer and quicken the pace of the game. What you're trying to do is get the players re-engaged.

After the scrimmage, you could have the players concentrate on individual skills, such as foul shooting, penalty kicks, serving, etc. Given sufficient time, you could move onto the next step in your practice plan. There will be days when the "best laid plans of mice and men" just don't seem to be working. This is not your fault. Be adaptable and keep your sense of humor. The bottom line is to have some additional items you could do at practice.

39 | Consequences

Being a coach is sometimes like being a parent. It's not a popularity contest and the players won't always like you. We've discussed using consequences as a way to keep practices focused and to add more pressure to drills. The thing to keep in mind is that there are good consequences and bad consequences.

You can always require the group that gets outperformed to do crunches, laps, or push-ups, but you can also promise positive consequences for good work. You can use food as a reward, or have the achieving players run fewer laps or do fewer crunches or push-ups. Whatever you choose, the point is to give your players some incentive to perform well in practice. Also, make sure that you enforce the consequences despite the inevitable grumbling that you will hear from the under-performing players. Tell them to try harder next time.

You can alternate the consequences in order to keep the players' attention. One thing that you need to remember about consequences is that it's important to make sure that every player has the possibility of success. Pair up the best players with those who need to improve.

40 | Praise in Public

Whatever you establish as your consequences, always recognize the efforts of the players at the conclusion of a difficult drill or intensive scrimmage. Give a shout out to the player or group that performs the best or demonstrates the qualities you're looking for. Always make sure that when you offer praise, the player or group of players deserves the recognition.

Set some rigid guidelines that your players must abide by in order to gain your praise. For young players, just a few positive words from you can last for weeks. Complimenting the players lets them know that you care and that you're paying attention to their efforts. Praising in public also lets the other players know exactly what you want them to do. If you find a player who has really mastered a skill, you might consider having him demonstrate that skill to the other players. A critical skill that you need to develop is to be able to recognize every player. Players appreciate an encouraging word.

41 | Chastise in Private

"To err is human" is a mantra that you should keep at the front of your mind as you coach. Have you ever been berated by a coach in front of the entire team? How did you feel? Have you ever watched the rest of the team as a player gets yelled at by the coach? All of the heads go down, feet are shuffling, it's very, very quiet, and do you know what the players are thinking? "Wow, am I ever glad that's not me!"

If a player has broken a team rule or displayed poor sportsmanship and needs to be disciplined or chastised, this should be done in private, away from the rest of the team. If it can wait until the next day, that's even better, as this will give you time to remove your emotions from the situation. If you feel that the situation needs to be addressed immediately, then take a deep breath, prepare yourself to unemotionally address the player, and move away from the team. Turn your back to the team and speak in a voice that only the player can hear. Explain that it is her action, attitude, or sportsmanship that you are addressing—you're not attacking the person, just what she's done wrong. If you feel that there needs to be a consequence, make sure that your punishment matches the deed. Once you have addressed the problem, forget it and move on. Going ballistic on a player in public only creates hard feelings and alienates the player from you.

42 | Take Advantage of Your Assistant Coach(es)

If you're lucky enough to have an assistant coach, make sure that you take full advantage of her help. When you create your practice plans, have drills or stations that she can run and coach. By having multiple stations running at the same time, you will be able to optimize your practice time, have fewer players standing around idly, and increase the number of touches each player gets during practice.

Solicit ideas from your assistant. Ask about her favorite drills. What were her strengths when she played? At times, your assistant may feel odd giving the "head coach" advice. Most likely, she will be a parent volunteer. Be persistent—the more ideas that you can gather, the better. And besides, asking for input does not necessarily mean that you will accept every idea offered.

Having an assistant also allows you to observe your team while someone else runs a drill or play, which gives you the opportunity to focus on your players' individual skills. If you find that a player needs one-on-one attention, you can pull her from the drill and work with her while the rest of the team continues the drill.

During games, have your assistant collect game statistics. Make the statistics meaningful by tracking what you have been working on in practice. With this information, you can give feedback to the team on how they are doing. If you don't like keeping statistics, then divide your team up between the two of you and observe the players on the field or court. You're observing to make sure that the players are playing as a

→

team and executing the plays that they've been practicing. Another thing that you should make sure of is that all of the players get a chance to touch the ball, rather than just stand still.

43 | Step Outside the Drill and Observe

As volunteer coaches, we have all likely spent time on the playing field or court (maybe even a lot of time). During practice there is, at times, an almost overwhelming urge to mix it up with the players. A hard lesson that I have begun to learn (more and more clearly as I become more and more youthfully challenged) is that, when I step in to demonstrate what a jock I am, my ability to observe the entire team in action is significantly reduced. I'm concentrating so hard on playing that I don't always see the players and how they are executing the fundamentals or plays that I have tried to teach them. Being able to step outside of the drill allows you to concentrate on all of the players; you will be able to closely observe and offer help to everyone. When you're observing, you can often take a player off to the side for individual instruction while the rest of the team continues the drill or play (as was mentioned in the last tip). If the team happens to be missing a player, you can ask your assistant to step in and play, or you might even enlist one of the parents to help out.

Game On

44 | First Game

This is what you've been working so hard for, it's game time! Before you get to the game, there are some things that you should take care of.

First of all, are playing jerseys or uniforms being supplied? If so, how will you take possession of them? Also, will you have to supply referee help? (Some of you may go, "Huh?" on this one, but for school volleyball, parents are often enlisted to help line judge and keep score.) It's important to be aware of what is required and to be prepared to fulfill your team duties.

It's a good idea to have the players arrive at the game site fifteen minutes early. There are a couple of reasons for this. For one thing, it allows the players some time to get ready and loosened up. Also, and this is more important for you, it allows you to know which players are available to play. It can be a real distraction if you're trying to adjust your lineup, get the players warmed up, and rework your substitutions one minute before game time. Encourage the players to take responsibility for getting to the game early.

45 | Lineups

Having your starting lineup and substitution list ready prior to game time will allow you to focus on what's happening in the game. Some coaches appear to keep their lineups and substitution lists in their heads. For many of us, that would result in having the wrong substitution order, putting players in the wrong positions, or worst of all, forgetting to put a player in the game (and it's rather embarrassing to tell parents that you forgot about their child!).

You will definitely need to know the league rules concerning substitutions. Some leagues require all players to play for at least half the game, while others require substitutions halfway through each quarter. You will need to know the rules and plan accordingly.

Developing your lineup in advance gives you some time to think about how you want to balance your lineups. On most teams, you will have a wide range of athletic abilities. Use what you've learned about your players in practice to build your lineups. Which players seem to work the best together? If all players are to get equal amounts of playing time, you might consider building a lineup composed of weaker and stronger players; if you play all of your strongest players in one lineup, you will have a less-talented group substituting into the game, which can make things very frustrating for both the players and you.

46 | Player Rotation

Tip #45 discussed knowing your local rules for substituting players, and tip #19 addressed personal competition philosophy. Even on the most competitive of teams, you'll need to make sure that all of your players get adequate playing time. No one likes just sitting on the bench, and substituting also gives your more skilled players a chance to rest and catch their breath. You can also talk to your players while they're on the bench—give them tips on how to play better or point out to them what is happening on the field or court.

Rotating players also gives your less-experienced players valuable playing time. Giving everyone a chance to play will prepare them for future games when (and I guarantee that this will happen) two or three of your starters are sick, hurt, or on family vacation and you need to come up with a different lineup than the one you usually use. Knowing what all of your players are capable of will help fill in the lineups when you're short-handed.

None of this is to say that every player must get the exact same amount of playing time; the point is that having a player sit on the bench all the time is doing a disservice to both that player and yourself. You can practice with a team all the time, but you won't really know what your players are capable of until they're faced with an opponent.

47 | It's About Having Fun

When the competitive juices get flowing and you're into the competition, it's difficult to step back and remember that you're the coach and the game is for the players. At one point during my coaching maturation process (which is still going on), I was a "screamer." I believed that if I yelled loud enough, the players would play better, and if I kept up a constant stream of what the players should be doing, then they would execute everything we had practiced. You might be wondering, "How can yelling make the players play better?" You're right to be cynical, because it won't! It took my daughter getting up in my face and telling me to back off to make things clear to me, and it was somewhat embarrassing. For some reason, I thought that part of being a coach was having total control and that yelling was part of that persona—like what you see on TV with some of the professional coaches, and even some of the college coaches. The problem is that the athletes that play for these types of coaches are highly trained, highly skilled, and those teams are playing to win. Those coaches are also being paid extremely high salaries to win (if you're being compensated, I would guess that it's not very much). Your team, Coach, on the other hand, is playing to learn, playing to develop, and most importantly, playing to have fun. Keep that in mind, step back, take a deep breath, and even laugh once in a while.

48 | Catch Them Doing Something Right

We spend what sometimes feels like countless hours teaching, demonstrating, diagramming, and practicing with our teams. When we see the "lights go on" and the players execute a play or demonstrate a higher-level skill to perfection, our chests expand a bit farther, we stand a tad taller and straighter, and we might even strut a little—we've done it! Unfortunately, it's only on rare days that this actually occurs. More likely, the players won't quite get what we're teaching, the plays that they're practicing are a stretch in relation to the experience level of the team, and we may at times even be convinced that there is a plot to thwart our plans.

So, what is the common response to all of this? First, we constantly remind our players of what they're *not* doing. We then tell them how well they're coming along, and then we tell them again what they're not doing or what they should be doing to make it perfect. The problem is that most players won't hear the compliment—the part that should make them feel good about themselves—but will only take in what they did wrong or the things that they need to do differently.

Rather than having your players constantly cringing as a result of waiting for the inevitable "but," try to catch them doing things right and point those out. Especially when things aren't going well or when the team has lost a game, the negativity and excuses can come fast and furious. Rather than focusing on the bad breaks or bad calls, focus on what the individual players and the team as a whole did right. You might have to take the lead on this the first couple of times, but the players will quickly get the idea and respond.

49 | Game Days

The type of team you're coaching will determine what should occur on game days. If this is a recreational league, just getting your players to the field or court early might be all that you need to worry about. If you coach a middle school or high school team, you might need to think about a pregame meal or snack.

For a school team, have the players gather after school or at a pre-arranged time, get into their uniforms, and come together as a team and start focusing on the game. If you're providing food, the players really don't need to eat a lot—just some calories to get their body engines going. Try to have the team finish eating an hour before the game. Meet with the players prior to warm-ups and talk to them about what you want them to focus on during the game. Have one or two specific objectives; if you have too many, the players will get confused. The notes that you take after games will help direct your thoughts. If you've seen the opponent play, you might offer specific advice about what to watch out for or any weaknesses that you noted.

For outdoor games such as soccer, baseball, or football, you'll need to make sure that there is plenty of water and cups available for the players. If you're coaching a school team, you'll need to pay the referees or umpires when you have home games. Find out who writes the checks and who presents payment to the officials, because it might be you.

50 | Keeping Stats

The importance of statistics for your team is something that only you can decide. For me, keeping stats during games is always of some value—it lets me see how each individual is performing and allows me to track the team's progress throughout the season. You might want to recognize individual players for outstanding performance, and stats can help you do that.

The difficult thing about keeping stats is deciding which categories should be tracked and then finding someone to record them. Coaching the team and keeping lineups straight while simultaneously keeping stats is more than most coaches can handle all at once.

If you decide to keep game stats, decide early on which ones you think are important and which ones you think can be ignored. You might want to surf the internet for stat sheets or browse some coaching books for suggested tracking sheets. When you've decided what you want to record, either ask your assistant coach to keep track of them or ask a parent to volunteer to help out. You might also consider rotating the recording duties among the parents so that no one person has to record all of the games.

The good thing about keeping stats is that it gives you hard data to reference after the game to help you assess what the team needs to work on. You might also consider having someone record the game for you on DVD, as this is an excellent way to assess what the team needs to work on. (I will warn you that watching these videos or DVDs can be addictive, and your significant other might not take kindly to you ignoring him or her to watch your team!)

51 | Prepare Your Substitution List in Advance

Lineups were already discussed previously, but the importance of preparing a substitution list in advance bears repeating. If your team only has one or two substitutes, then you can probably skip this tip.

Without having a sub list prepared, it is really difficult to watch the game, coach your players, call plays, and decide within thirty seconds or less who will sub in for whom. During the timeout or substitution break, you can use the time (usually only a minute) to focus on coaching and talking to your team, rather than fumbling with paper and pen and scratching out lineups.

Preparing your sub list early also allows you to create more effective lineups, as you can maximize your players' strengths and match up players who have complementary skills. Pairing up players and skills that mesh well together requires some thought, so take time to prepare this before the game.

52 | The Players Just Don't Get It

You've practiced the drills and run the plays during practice and now you feel confident that the team can perform them in the game. The game starts and you can't wait to see your team blow the doors off the competition. Here it comes—your team is in position to strut its stuff. But, what the heck? What's going on? No one on the team appears to have the slightest idea what it is you want them to do! Even worse, no one on the team seems to have any desire to attempt to execute.

Always keep in mind that this type of situation isn't the result of a conspiracy by your players to make you look bad, nor are they trying to get even with you for making them run suicides. Chances are that the players are so pumped up with adrenaline and the thrill of competition that they are rendered almost incapable of concentrating on what you've been practicing or thinking about what they should be doing. Younger players especially get so excited that they just can't control themselves.

So, do you throw up your hands and give up? No. First, let them play for a few minutes and see if they start to calm down and play the way you practiced. If things continue to resemble a rugby scrum, call a timeout. You don't have to yell—just talk to the players and remind them of what they've been practicing. Tell them that you know that there's a perfect execution just waiting to happen, but only if they work together as a team.

53 | Timeouts

Some sports, such as soccer and baseball, don't have official timeouts; however, all sports allow some kind of time for you to talk to your players, encourage them, and remind them of what you want them to do. For example, in baseball, you can talk to your players while they're at bat. You can also use substitutions to your advantage by having the subs tell the other players what you want them to concentrate on.

If you're coaching a sport such as basketball or volleyball that does have official timeouts, use them. Keep in mind, however, that timeouts are not cumulative—you can't store them or carry them over to the next game. If the players are really playing hard and appear to be getting tired, call a timeout to allow them to catch their breath. Timeouts also allow you to encourage your players, tell them what you want them to do, and point things out that might have escaped their minds. Use the time to be positive.

Another use of the timeout is sort of obvious—the other team is on a run and starting to pull away. Use the timeout to refocus your players, calm them down, and give yourself an opportunity to help them step up their play. This might even disrupt the flow of the other team and knock them off their stride.

54 | How to Keep Them Loose

As players get into the teenage years, the intensity and pressure of the games will increase. There will come times—tournament games or rival matches—when players are edgy, out-of-sorts, and apparently unable to calm down. The pressure of the moment starts to bother them, which can affect the way they play. It's your job to loosen the players up and allow them to play like you know they can.

Your players will often take their cues from you. Are you acting differently than you normally do? Are you short-tempered? Is your coaching demeanor different? If it's a championship game, remind them that there are lots of other teams that haven't made it this far. Try to put the game into perspective. What are the players going to remember twenty years from now? Most likely, it will be that they got to play in the big game, so tell them to make it as memorable as possible. If you notice the players getting tense during the game, use your timeouts. Have the players take deep breaths and remind them of why they are in the game and what has made them successful to this point.

What else can you do? You might consider looking up corny jokes or knock-knock jokes, and if you think it's appropriate, tell one during timeout. Even a bad joke can relieve the tension and allow the players to focus on playing.

55 | Patience

At this point, you might think that I'm paranoid about conspiracies and the idea of players planning to make you look bad. There will come a time when you've tried everything to get your point across and it just doesn't appear to be sinking in. You've spent what you consider to be an inordinate amount of time planning, organizing, and developing your strategy. It's good, and you get it, and you just don't understand why your players don't get it. Of course it can't be you—it's got to be them! They weren't so thick-headed during the last practice, so what gives now?

If you step back and think about it a bit, you should begin to see all of this more clearly. Think about how you learned to ride a bicycle. You started with a tricycle, then moved up to a bike with training wheels, and finally graduated to a two-wheeler, which was initially a little wobbly. Now, transfer that over to your players. They're just beginning their journeys toward becoming athletes—the two-wheeler is still wobbly.

At times, you'll notice that enthusiasm is lacking and no one seems to care about what's going on or remember a single thing from practice. Watching your team play when this is the case can be painful. When you step back and review the entire season, you'll see that the players have progressed in steps (sometimes two steps forward and one step back). In the end, the players usually arrive at the point that you wanted them to, so don't give up.

56 | Capture Your Thoughts After the Game

Win or lose, after the game, try to take five or ten minutes to review what happened. Write your impressions down while the game is fresh in your memory and try not to get hung up on whether the team won or lost. The final score is of less importance than your impressions of how your players performed. How did they exhibit their individual skills? Did they play as a team? Did your players execute the plays that they had practiced? Did they appear to be having fun?

As you write your thoughts down, think about what you want to say to the team. It's a good idea to share these thoughts with your team at the next practice. You might consider asking them for their impressions of the game before offering your feedback. What do they think they did well and what might they work on to improve? After getting their impressions, tell them what they did well and then remind them of what they need to work on, and make sure to praise the players who demonstrated what you think is most important. Taking notes will also enable you to develop more effective practice plans, as you can spend time concentrating on what the team and players need to do to get better.

Building a Team

57 | Team Bonding Thoughts

Because the next four or five tips address team bonding, they might not apply to you if you're coaching a recreation team.

When you first select players for the team, you'll probably have a diverse set of individuals—some will have played together before, some will be best friends, some will be from different schools or grade levels, and some will be total strangers to the rest of the players. Part of the coach's job is to mold the group into a cohesive team. The process should begin either during the preseason or shortly after the season starts.

Team bonding seems very simple, and trying to plan activities that are directly targeted toward team building might seem unnecessary. Also, everyone is busy with jobs, school, and practice, so adding another activity can feel like overkill. So why is team bonding important?

It's important to let everybody meet and get to know each other in a non-competitive and non-sports-related environment (especially younger players, who should have a chance to become acquainted with and accepted by the older players). In this context, the players won't try to impress each other, but will instead relax and just get to know one another. If you're coaching a school team, your goal should be to break down the grade level barriers.

Bonding activities can last a couple of hours or can be overnight events. It's about the players—you, as the coach, are not required to attend. If you are going to attend, plan on being there for only a short time. It's important to let the players socialize without a coach watching over them. You'll need to coordinate these events with a couple of the players' parents.

58 | Sleepover

The sleepover is a bonding activity that tends to be more popular with girls, although boys might enjoy it as well. Getting the players together for an overnight activity will require some planning and cooperation from the parents (and of course, the approval of all of the other parents). The goal is to get everyone together, but coordinating everyone's schedule is sometimes impossible. Ask around and book the date that will have the best player turnout.

Let the players help plan the activity. If you want to include something to get them thinking about the sport, you might consider bringing a video of a professional game or maybe an instructional video on some key aspect of the sport. Something else you might want to consider is a sports movie (*Hoosiers* and *Rudy* come to mind as inspirational options).

With the extended time allowed by a sleepover, you can have the team do group activities, such as tie-dying T-shirts or coming up with team cheers (one team I coached came up with a rap song for the team—it was hilarious!). Whatever you choose to do, the point is to get the players working together in a fun environment.

59 | Bowling

Maybe a sleepover feels like a bit much, or maybe the team is too dispersed for it to be feasible. If that's the case, then getting together to go bowling is an excellent alternative. Bowling is a fun activity that everyone can participate in (and most bowling alleys have bumpers that can be inflated so that the gutters are covered and pins will be knocked down every time).

You might consider pairing up new players with returning players or younger players with older ones. You could also swap partners every five frames or every game so that everyone gets to meet and play with new people. Try to avoid allowing friends to partner up and exclude other players—this will help avoid the formation of cliques. Stop for something to eat and drink along the way or after you're done.

60 | Team Dinner

Having dinner is another idea for a team bonding activity. Going to a restaurant doesn't always allow the players to mingle and introduce themselves, so a good idea is to have a pot luck dinner at someone's home. Have each family bring one food item to the dinner, as this tends to be much less expensive than bringing everyone to a restaurant. Also, being in a low-key home environment will allow the players, parents, and coach(es) to mingle. As a coach, it will give you the chance to meet all of the parents outside of the sports venue. You can use "ice breaker" games to get things started and get everyone involved. The internet is a treasure trove of fun games to play with people who don't necessarily know each other.

61 | Attend a "Higher-Level" Game as a Team

If the sport you coach has a higher-level team, such as a high school, college, or professional team, then you might consider having your team attend a game together. Having your team watch more skilled and experienced players is really valuable. Sit with them and point out things that they can work on, and when you see teams executing fundamentals, make sure that your players see it. Also, ask your players to point out things that are similar to what they do and tell them that they can reach that level of play if they work hard.

If you're coaching a grade school or middle school team, consider attending a high school game. Your players might know some of the athletes, and if you know the coach, ask him or her to come and talk to your team—your players will enjoy meeting a "higher-level" coach. If you're lucky enough to have colleges and universities nearby, you might be able to take your team to games for free.

62 | Things to Try at Practice to Build "Team"

Running endless drills, scrimmaging, doing stretches, and conditioning starts to get a bit stale after about the fourth or fifth time, and players can become a bit lax in their execution of any or all of these as a result. Activities like those discussed in tip #34 are great for giving your practices variety and getting your team used to relying on each other for help.

63 | It's Not Always About Wins and Losses

If you explained to your players that yours is a "play-to-win" team at the beginning of the season, then you can skip over this tip. If you're coaching a younger team (up to eighth grade), then give this tip some thought.

Winning is a great experience. It builds confidence and self esteem and looks great on your resume. On the other hand, winning can come at the expense of player development. Usually, you'll have a core group of skilled players while the rest of the team is made up of players with less experience and developing skills. To maximize your players' development, you might have to sacrifice winning. Players can scrimmage in practice, but there's no replacement for the competitive game. Giving every team member playing time in the actual game gives them a chance to experience what a thrill it is to play. Remember that playing is a privilege, not an entitlement. If your school team plays non-conference games, you might consider giving your less-experienced players more time on the field or court. Of course, you can play to win during conference games, but even then, make sure that all of the players get into the game.

There is a definite upside to doing this, and that is that the younger players who return the next season will have gained valuable playing experience and will be ready to step into the starting role for you, and it's all because you took the time to develop them!

64 | When Your Players Want to Fight Back

There will be games in which the other team is much more aggressive and physical than your team; in fact, your opponent may even play to a point that you consider "dirty." Your players will probably discover this earlier than you will. You might hear during timeouts that the other team is playing dirty or being unsportsmanlike. Tell them right then that you expect them not to lower themselves to unsportsmanlike play.

As you observe the way your team plays, you might start to notice some of your players acting more aggressively than you'd like. At that point, it's time to step in and tell them exactly what you expect from them. Sportsmanship and clean play are the standards that they are held to, and any deviation from those standards will have consequences. Tell them that poor sportsmanship will get them a spot on the bench next to you until they get the point.

If you have players who tend to play dirty from the outset, nip that in the bud. Pull the player immediately and tell her that that kind of behavior is unacceptable and that she will only return to the game when she can play according to the rules.

65 | What to do About Cliques

You're likely to encounter players who are friends from school or their neighborhoods. It's important to make sure that these friends don't exclude other players. Cliques are especially common in school teams with players of different ages and grade levels. To establish and build team spirit with your players, you'll have to minimize the effects of cliques. One way to do this is to not allow the cliques to warm up together exclusively. A method of doing this is to carry white poker chips that are numbered from 1 to the number of players on the team. Pass the chips out and pair the players up according to number groups or sequences (for example, put even numbers against odds). This way, you'll end up with more random groups.

To further reduce the effect of cliques, have the older players choose younger partners. This also helps the players get to know each other. You can also have the more skilled and experienced players pair up with those who need some help. Tell the older players that they need to be able to teach and lead their partners, cheer them on, and help them improve.

If you notice that cliques are starting to affect the team's unity and ability to play together as a group, then consider having a team meeting. Tell your players that you expect them to work with everyone. If this doesn't work, talk to the players individually and tell them that there are consequences for not playing as a team.

Parents

66 | Communication Is Critical

Communication is critical for your players, their parents, and your sanity. Having open lines of communication will avoid misunderstandings and hurt feelings.

Keeping parents involved makes them a part of the team, and you need their cooperation and support in order to have an enjoyable season. Begin your communication with them early and continue communicating with them throughout the season. At the beginning of the preseason, meet with the parents and lay out your expectations. Tell them what you expect from the players and what they can expect you to teach their children. Also, let them know that you'll be taking notes on your impressions of each player, as this will allow you to discuss their strengths and areas of improvement, should the parents ask. Suggest to them that, if they want to talk to you, before and after practice are good times to do so in order for them to get undivided attention (right after a game isn't really the best time for this—attempting to have an unemotional discussion about things like playing time right after competition may have disastrous results). Ask the parents to be good sports and to cheer for the team.

Stress that being early to practices and games is necessary, as the players need time to get ready and warm up. When you receive the season's schedule, make sure that everyone has a copy and provide directions to practice or game venues.

It's very important to repeat, repeat, and repeat—this will guarantee that everyone hears the same message.

67 | Request a Team Parent

Team parents are lifesavers and stress relievers. The role of the team parent is to assist with all of the administrative tasks required to keep the team functioning smoothly. Email addresses, telephone calling trees, snack schedules, and weekly practice and game day reminders are just a few of the things that the team parent can do for you. He or she can also inform you of which players will and will not be attending practices and games.

A team parent can also act as a conduit for providing feedback to you. Some parents feel uneasy about expressing dissenting views or complaints, and having the team parent act as a third party helps some people express their views. With the team parent you are freed from worrying about the minutiae of keeping tabs on everyone and everything that needs to be done.

68 | Add an Assistant Coach

You might have just read that title and thought, "I think I've read this before." You're partially correct—earlier tips did discuss the assistant coach. It's reappearing here because having an assistant coach or even a parent to help you with practices and games will make your life much easier and enable you to do things with your team that would be nearly impossible without help.

Because having an assistant allows you to run concurrent drills and provide more one-on-one instruction to all of the players, you will be able to extend what you do at practices to include more touches for the players. During games, you'll be able to provide additional coaching to the players on the bench, as you'll have a second set of eyes watching the players on the field or court and, if you choose, keeping stats.

Because most of us have full-time jobs and families, our time is at a premium. It's not an admission of some failing or lack of skill on your part to say that you need help, it's just good common sense. If you can make your life simpler and less stressful, why not?

69 | Meet With Your Assistant Coach One-on-One

If you're fortunate enough to have a parent volunteer to help you coach, it's a good idea to sit down and talk one-on-one before the season starts (face-to-face is great, but over the phone works as well). You want to make sure that you're compatible in your thinking and approach to the game. Find out a little bit about your assistant's background and favorite hobbies, etc. Get to know her and discuss your expectations. You didn't ask her to just show up and babysit, did you?

Ask your assistant about her playing and coaching experience, approach to competition, and expectations. Discuss practice and how you would like to run them, ask about her favorite drills, and talk about how to handle difficult players. Also, go over the schedule of practices and games and make sure that your assistant is available to cover for you on any dates on which you'll be unavailable. You and your assistant can become a "dynamic duo," and you'll find yourself able to relax and enjoy being a coach.

70 | Your Coaching Philosophy

When I first started to develop my own personal coaching philosophy, I laughed because, as I thought about all of the coaches that I had growing up, I realized that not a single one ever shared his philosophy with the team. I know that things have changed a great deal since I played sports (my kids jokingly ask if I competed in the very first Olympics), but as I continue to refine my philosophy, I find that it really helps to put it into words.

Every coach will have a different philosophy, which will vary depending on age, skill level, and competitive level of the league. Developing a coaching philosophy will make you think about what your approach to the sport really is. The key is that, once you've developed a philosophy, you should share it with the players and parents. Why? Because sharing your coaching philosophy provides insight into you as the coach, what your priorities are, and how you approach the game.

Your philosophy doesn't have to be a detailed thesis (besides, if it's too long, no one will read the entire thing). Six to ten sentences should be about the right length. Have a look at the volleyball coaching philosophy in the appendix for an example.

71 | Set Your Expectations for the Parents

It's very important to share a few basic thoughts with the players' parents early in the season. Some suggested discussion items are:

- Playing time: Is this a play-for-fun team, or is this a play-to-win team? This will determine how much playing time each player receives.
- Arrival time: When do you want the players to arrive for practice and games?
- Sportsmanship: How do you expect the players to behave toward each other and opponents?
- Etiquette: How do you expect the parents to behave at games? (This is a good time to discourage yelling at officials.)
- Issues: When are the best times for parents to contact you if they have a question or issue?
- Homework: Encourage the parents to work with their children outside of practice.
- Assistance: How can the parents help at practice?

It's very important that you talk with the parents early on in the season in order to help them understand your approach to the game, as this can help avoid unnecessary conflicts later on in the season.

72 | Your Thoughts on Parental "Help"

Have you ever been to a game and seen a player receiving instructions from both the coach and a parent at the same time? The poor kid usually looks confused and lost. Every child wants to please his parents and do what he's told. Unfortunately, the playing field isn't a very good place to try to do what the parent wants, especially if the coach wants something different.

You want to encourage the parents to cheer heartily for their children and the team, but you also want them to understand that you are the coach and the players need to listen to you. The players can't listen to you if they're trying to listen to their parents ("A house divided"...you get the point). You might also want to discuss help during practice with the parents. Some parents have an overwhelming urge to get out on the practice field and compete; they want to show the kids what a jock they are and how well they can play the game. There are a couple of problems with this. The first problem is safety, for both the parent and the players. The parents are usually larger and stronger and could injure the players by hitting the ball too hard or physically running into them while trying to make a shot. Also, parents are usually not properly stretched out and warmed up, which makes them more susceptible to injury, which creates a liability issue. The second problem is that parents who participate in this way will likely interfere with practice and what you're trying to work on.

Asking the parents early in the season to avoid coming onto the field avoids interference later on. You can ask for parental help if you need it, but make sure that they understand that you will ask them for it first. If the group wants to have a parents versus players night, that's fine, just schedule this for late in the season and have a fun night.

73 | Solicit Ideas for Practice

As was mentioned earlier, don't feel like you have to be the encyclopedia for everything related to your sport. Ask the parents for their ideas and input, including their favorite drills, competitions and games, and plays. Aside from giving you great ideas for practice, getting parents involved in this way makes you appear approachable, which opens up and encourages two-way communication.

Don't think that you have to use everything that the parents suggest. Use your good judgment and be diplomatic, and make sure to thank them. You might even consider acknowledging input that you receive in front of the other parents and players—everyone likes to be praised.

Another valuable thing to ask parents is how they think the team is playing. Remember, though, to take this input with a grain of salt, as most parents will just concentrate on their own children (even so, it never hurts to ask). Tell the parents exactly what you'd like them to watch out for and whether it's offense or defense that you'd like feedback on. As the coach, it's sometimes difficult to accurately assess how your team is playing just by watching. The point of view of a parent, coach, or teacher is just another resource to help you coach.

74 | Handling the "Over-the-top" Parent

Regardless of the age and skill level of the players that you're coaching, at some point in your coaching career, you might run into an "over-the-top" parent. What are you going to do when one of your parents is shouting at the top of his lungs (and not in a way that serves to cheer the team on)? What about a parent who appears to be headed toward the opponent's bench after yelling throughout the entire game that they played dirty or targeted his child? Or how about the parent who is constantly and obnoxiously berating the officials? Maybe you've witnessed this personally.

As sports become more competitive, demanding, and intense, parents are becoming increasingly overwhelmed by and obsessed with the idea of their child's team winning. They appear to be unable to control themselves. So what do you do? The unwanted behavior needs to be addressed; otherwise it will persist and probably get worse. It's probably not a good idea to confront the parent immediately after the game unless he appears to be headed for trouble. Talk to him at the next practice or, if you think the problem needs to be addressed quickly, later on the same day. Take a deep breath and calm yourself, and when you talk to the parent, make sure he understands that you're criticizing his actions, rather than him personally. The conversation needs to be controlled and non-threatening.

Many referees are now able to penalize the team and coach of the offending parent. Make sure he is aware of this and remind him that you do not want your team to be banned from the field or made to lose. This is something that should be addressed early in the pre-season, before games even begin. Remind everyone that they're representing the team, the club or school, and maybe even the city.

75 | When Parents Disagree with Their Child's Playing Time

Parents are often unable to objectively evaluate their children's abilities, so why should your players' parents be any different? At some point, you'll be approached by a parent who believes that his child is the next Michael Jordan or Mia Hamm and that you're not playing him or her enough or in the right position. Take heart, as you're definitely not the first to be confronted, nor will you be the last.

You'll first need to consider whether or not the parent is actually correct. Ask yourself, is there some reason that you're consciously or unconsciously not playing his child? Assuming that you're not on a vendetta to punish the player, stop and think about how your team is set up. This is where keeping stats, taking notes after games, and hanging onto tryout evaluations come in handy. What are the strengths and weaknesses of the player in question? Discuss this with the parent and suggest drills for the player to focus on. Keep the discussion centered on the specific player, rather than on the rest of the team or other players. Thank the parent for coming to talk with you and encourage him to continue to do so when necessary. If the parent is concerned that his child is playing the wrong position, review your philosophy of your team's setup. Most importantly, be friendly and respectful.

76 | Avoid Comparing Players

In team sports, parents will inevitably compare their children to the other players on the team (or even to players on other teams). As the coach, you should avoid this type of discussion at all costs. Comparing players serves no constructive purpose and will most likely come back to haunt you later— misstated, misunderstood, and misinterpreted. Instead, focus on the specifics for each individual player, such as what they do to help the team and how they can work to improve their game.

Let both your team and the parents know that players can differentiate themselves in a number of ways. Practicing ethics and working hard during each practice (this is where the "practice like you'd play in the game" mantra comes in) will help players set themselves apart. Working on skills outside of practice, displaying a team attitude, cheering for fellow teammates, and being generally positive all indicate maturity and will ultimately set players apart from one another.

77 | Ask for Feedback

Throughout the season, take a minute or two at the beginning or end of a practice to talk with the parents. Ask them how their child is enjoying the season and if there's anything that you could be doing better.

Solicit this input regularly throughout the season and attempt to talk to every child's parent at least once. Often, the response you'll receive is that everything is fine and you're doing a good job. Be persistent and don't rest on the first "nice job" you receive. Not everyone is used to being asked for input, and by being proactive, you can often avoid being blindsided at the end of the season by a parent who's been on a slow boil throughout the entire season over a perceived offense. Once the parents see that you're sincere and working to improve, they'll become more relaxed, offer suggestions, and be even more receptive to your requests.

Sportsmanship

78 | Referees Are Human, Too

Game officials are some of the most abused, berated, and disliked people around. It's so much easier to transfer our anger over the team's inability to perform onto a third party, and the closest third party is usually the referee or umpire. More often than I'd like, I read about an irate parent accosting a referee in the national paper. Considering the magnitude of these parents' reactions, you'd think the NBA or NFL championship was on the line. No wonder the referee ranks are dwindling.

I won't pretend that I've always been a "friend of the referee." I'll admit that I've done my share of complaining and carping. As I've aged, however, it has occurred to me that these are people who, like the coaches and parents, have a deep love of the game and volunteer to help it gain popularity. Whatever pay they receive certainly doesn't offset the poor treatment that they receive. Do they make mistakes? Of course they do! Unfortunately, in our leagues, we don't have the advantage of instant replays or an entire staff of referees (sometimes we're lucky to have one!). So lighten up on the referees and treat them with respect and dignity. Demand this of yourself, your players, and your parents.

79 | Referees Also Need Practice

Here's something that isn't earth-shattering but might not have occurred to you. How does a referee get to be competent and respected in his sport? By attending classes, taking tests, and most of all, through lots of practice. Just as you're trying to get your players to perform at a higher level through practice, game officials improve by actually officiating games. Have you ever tried to learn how to do something by just watching a video or reading a book? Sooner or later, you need to actually perform whatever it is that you're trying to learn. The case is the same for officials.

You could contact your local area game official scheduler early in your preseason training and ask if they would be interested in having an education session for the referees. You can host the night and hold a practice game. You might even invite another school to scrimmage. This way, you'll create good will with the officials, they'll get much-needed practice, and everyone will move forward.

80 | Your Players are Watching You

If you're a parent, you learned very early in your child's life that children watch and listen to you like hawks. Have you ever watched your children play pretend, and then been astonished when you hear your own words, perfectly inflected, coming out of their mouths? They might not be able to pronounce many words, but they sure can be crystal clear (and usually very loud) with the four-letter words!

What's the point here? Just like your children, your players are watching you. Are you fair to them all the time? Do you hold every player to the same standards, or do you allow the "stars" to slough off during conditioning or running? Do you preach sportsmanship, yet still yell at the officials or the opposing coach? Your players will take their cues from you; however you act and react, they're likely to do the same.

You might start to hear them make excuses for why they lost, including bad calls, poor officiating, or dirty play by the other team. When you hear things like this, it's time to consider how you act in front of your team. It might not even be you—it could be a result of how they've been coached in the past or taught to act by their parents. Regardless, talk to your team and make it very clear that poor sportsmanship is unacceptable. Start by demonstrating good sportsmanship and "walking the walk."

81 | What About all of the Other Points That Were Scored?

There are bound to be games in which it appears that every close call goes against your team. When this happens, it can seem like the fates as well as the officials are conspiring against you. Your players might be devastated and probably very angry. This is an excellent opportunity for you to teach them something.

How you handle a situation like this will go a long way toward helping your players become good sports and, more importantly, good people. You can say, "Life sucks, and the refs blew it," or, you can take a different approach and talk about all of the other points that were or were not scored during the game. Were there times earlier in the game at which the players were not quite playing to their potential? Were shots missed because someone was lazy in execution? Was the team more focused on the officials than on executing what you practiced? Get the players to focus on what the team could have done to avoid a situation in which officials might influence the game.

82 | Life's Lessons: Bad Call, Lost Game—It's Not Always Fair

What's even worse than losing because of unprofessional or poorly-trained officials is losing due to a game-deciding call (especially when you're playing your rival). What will really send you into orbit is when, after the game, the head official tells you that they blew the call! It's enough to make you want to swear!

As unpleasant as it is, this situation presents another opportunity for you to work with your players and help them grow into strong adults. Rather than blaming the officials and bemoaning the loss, tell the players (after they've kept their heads up and acted like good sports) that you're proud of them and how they played. This is very difficult, and you probably want to scream, but now is not the time. Tell your players that life is not always fair and that things don't always work out. The upside is that it's just a game—no one was hurt, life goes on, and there will be another practice the next day. So what if it was the final game or the championship? There are lots of other teams that wished that they had even had the opportunity to play in the big game.

83 | When the Game's a Massacre

It's possible that you'll coach teams that fall on either side of the "massacre" scale. Sometimes, the other team will be so superior in skill, experience, and physicality that you'll be over-matched right from the start. You'll notice your players start to give up and you'll realize that there really isn't anything that they can do to avoid getting creamed. So what can you do?

Call timeouts, talk with the players, and have them focus on smaller victories instead of winning the game. Maybe it's just getting the basketball past half-court without turning the ball over, or maybe its scoring a run in baseball. Whatever the game is, work to keep their heads held high. Tell them that it's not about the final score, but it's about how they played. Yes, it might sound a little "preachy," but having the players concentrate can only help them become better players. You might also talk to the players on the bench and have them note what the other team is doing that your team could aspire to do.

Those are some ideas for what to do when you're on the "short end" of the game, but what happens when you realize immediately after the game starts that your team is far better than the opponent? Winning by a landslide doesn't really do anything for either team. Once your team is ahead and the outcome is evident, try rotating your players into different positions, or make them execute five extra passes before anyone can try to score. You can also use this opportunity to make sure that your substitutes get to play for longer than usual. If you can slow the play down to avoid scoring, tell your team to play at a slower pace—no fast breaks, no stolen bases, no breakaways, etc.

Always treat the other team with respect. I've thanked coaches who have done these things for my teams and I've been thanked by other coaches for doing the same.

84 | Controlling Attitudes

A team will start having problems quickly if the players start developing bad attitudes. Bad attitudes can take many forms, including cliques excluding players, individual players not hustling during practice, and players blaming each other for lost points or games. If allowed to continue, all of the players will eventually adopt these destructive attitudes.

Part of being a good coach is treating every player, from the superstar to the ultimate benchwarmer, exactly the same. If the players sense that you're playing favorites or cutting the better players more slack, they'll start to expect the same treatment. Be even-handed—if you set up consequences at the beginning of the season for being late or missing practice, make sure that you follow through for every player. If that means that a starting player has to miss a game or sit out for half of one, then that's what should happen— they were aware of the consequences and it's your responsibility to enforce them. The players will lose respect for you and wonder why they should work hard for you if you don't mean what you say.

Watch your players interact with each other before, during, and after practice. If you see any bullying or hazing (especially of the younger players), step in immediately and take action. In order to avoid embarrassing the offending player, do this one-on-one. Remember: it's the action, not the athlete, that's offensive. When you're observing your players, ask yourself: Are all of the players interacting? Are they practicing as a team? Is everyone involved in the conditioning and drills? If you've set the expectation that all players are to be involved, make sure that they're aware of this and the consequences for not participating. Name-calling, hazing, and ignoring teammates are signs of trouble. Be observant and try to stop these actions from having a negative effect on your team.

85 | Give Your Players Feedback at Least Once During the Season

Everyone likes to be told how they're doing, and your players are no different. To spark the players' drive and help them move to the next level, you'll want to provide them with feedback.

Talk to each player one-on-one, away from other players and parents, for about two to five minutes. Discuss what you like about the player, her strengths, and what areas could use more focus and practice. Give her specific drills or activities that she could do to improve. If there are mental areas (such as focus, concentration, and sportsmanship) that your player could work on, make sure to cover those areas as well. When you meet with the player, make sure that she understands that you're talking about her performance and attitude, rather than about her personality; making sure that the conversation doesn't come off as a personal attack will help her to better listen to and understand your feedback.

If you've taken the time to record your thoughts at tryouts and after games and practices, then you'll have a good start on player notes, which will make your feedback sessions go smoothly.

86 | Tell the Parents What You Told Their Child

Once you've talked with the players, take a moment to talk with one or both of their parents. You might even consider having parents actually attend their children's feedback sessions. If you meet with them separately, do so shortly after the session with the players—you want to make sure that they hear the same things that you said to their children, and this will help to avoid "he said, she said" misunderstandings. Many of the players will only hear half of what you say and might not fully understand your suggestions, so talking to the parents helps ensure that the things that you want the players to work on are noted and understood.

87 | Coaching Boys and Girls

As a society, we've come light years in our treatment of men's and women's sports. Title 9 has greatly improved the availability of scholarship money for women at the collegiate level, which has led to an increase in the number of young women competing in sports. The numbers continue to rise.

If you're coaching a team of young ladies for the first time, there are some differences between coaching boys and coaching girls that you should be aware of. It's been my experience that, if a guy isn't hustling or is lackluster in intensity during a game, you can call him over and read him the riot act. You can even raise your voice. He'll most likely look at you, nod, and go back into the game, and five minutes later, you'll probably be high-fiving and celebrating with him. Everything is forgotten and there's no grudge.

With a young woman, you might benefit from taking a more low-key approach. First, girls tend not to respond well when you get "nose-to-nose" with them, as they tend to be more sensitive about their personal space than boys are. Secondly, female players seem more likely to interpret harsh criticism as a personal attack. When you address attitudes or actions in a way that can be perceived as harsh, young ladies might take this personally, and when someone starts to feel attacked in this way, you've lost them—they'll withdraw and stop listening. If you see that this is happening with a player, step back and take a different approach. You'll find that this is a much easier path, as it will keep your players much happier.

Administrivia

88 | When Games are Canceled

Game cancellations are rare and occur more frequently with outdoor sports than with indoor ones. Even so, it's a good idea to be prepared for the rare occasions when things conspire to cancel a game.

The easiest way to be prepared is, if your league has a game hotline, to make sure that everybody has the number for it. Someone will eventually call you directly, but if you anticipate a cancellation, you should check regularly in order to find out as soon as possible. If there's not a hotline, think about having a phone calling tree (that is, you call the first two families, they each call two families, and so forth until everyone has been contacted). This will save you a lot of time.

It's a good idea to have your team parent build a telephone list that includes the parents' home and cell numbers. If it will fit, have the list printed on paper that's about the size of a playing card so that you can have it laminated and it will fit in a wallet.

89 | Handling Overnight Trips

If you're coaching a team that plays in tournaments that require overnight stays, there's quite a bit of planning and organization to do. Identify the weekends that your team will be playing out of town as early in the season as possible and work with your team parent on deciding where the team will stay. Having everyone stay at the same hotel together is great for team building. Encourage everyone to get to the hotel as early as possible so that everyone will get a good night's rest (it's really hard to get players awake and playing hard for 8 a.m. games if everyone got to bed after eleven the night before).

There will probably be time during the weekend when no games are scheduled and you'll have blocks of down time. Find out what activities are available to do. Museums, aquariums, and city tours are all great for getting people out of the hotel and making them forget about competition for a little while. Playing putt-putt, taking advantage of the hotel pool (if applicable), and getting everyone together for a team dinner are always enjoyable. Also, the Wii and other video games allow everyone to get together and make great memories (and seeing the coach work the guitar in Rock Band can be downright hilarious).

90 | Tournaments

Tournaments are great events, even when they're local. Whenever possible (and whenever cost permits), enter your team into tournaments and talk to your players and their parents about them during your first meeting. It's possible that not everyone will be able to attend, but if there's enough interest, it's a great experience for the players. Check to see if there are local tournaments or some held in a city that you could make a day trip to in order to avoid the overnight expense.

Also, ask other coaches for recommendations regarding tournaments. Playing in one early in the season will allow you and your players to get a feel for how the team plays together. Tournaments toward the end or after the season are also valuable, as they allow the team to see how far they've progressed over the season. A tournament can also serve as a reward for the players; it's fun to compete against teams from across the state or out-of-state.

91 | Controlling the Tension

We've all been there—your palms are sweaty, your heart is racing, and you can't sit still. You're getting keyed up for the game and feeling that added burst of adrenaline. Players are usually surprised the first couple of times that they experience this sensation because they don't really understand what's happening to their bodies. Each of your players is unique and will react to tension differently.

The players will probably mimic your handling of tension to some extent. Do they see you doing things that are outside of your normal routine? Is your tension evident? Are you acting differently? If you've established a pregame routine, try and adhere to it—kids love routine, even if they tell you otherwise, and it keeps them focused. Tell the players that tension is a normal part of competition. Before the game, ask if anyone is nervous and be sure to raise your own hand. Let them know that the way they deal with tension could help decide the game. It's good to be excited—they just need to channel that excitement, focus, and play like they've practiced.

92 | "Results Anxiety"

For young players and even professional athletes, there will be games or events in which they appear to be in some kind of trance. The plays might have been perfect during practice, but now they're not being executed at all. Everyone seems hesitant and no one is stepping up to lead the team.

Young players are often worried about making mistakes, disappointing the coach, not being perfect, or looking foolish in front of friends and family. Welcome to "results anxiety." The players want to play well and win so badly that they become paralyzed. The good news is, the problem isn't you, so you can exhale. At this point, you need to get the players to believe in themselves just as much as you believe in them. Remind them that they've executed the same plays very well in practice, so they're completely capable of doing the same thing during a game. Just keep encouraging them. When your players are struggling with results anxiety, have them close their eyes and visualize a time at which they played their best—that time when the passes were crisp, the plays were well-run, and they scored. Once it's in their mind's eye, they're more likely to hold it and feel more comfortable on the field or court.

93 | Playing Everyone

For most players, playing in games is the primary reason to be involved in a sport, so playing time bears further discussion. As the coach, you're the ultimate decision maker in terms of who plays and for how long (if one of the players is your child, your job might be a little bit harder in this regard). Having guidelines for playing time set forth by the league will make your job a lot easier; however, not all leagues do this work for you.

When you selected your team at the beginning of the season, you picked players who you thought would make some kind of contribution. Sitting on the bench, as it turns out, doesn't make for much of a contribution. If your team is a competitive, play-to-win team, playing time probably won't be evenly distributed among all of the players; however, using all of the players effectively will benefit the team. Giving your better players time to rest will help them stay fresh and relaxed and will allow the other players to develop their skills.

94 | Get Together to Recognize the Team

When the season is over, it's fun to have the players and their families get together for an end-of-season celebration. This doesn't have to be an extravagant affair. If you're coaching a school team, you might be able to hold the event at school. You could have each family bring a covered dish, you could order pizza, or you could just have a dessert meeting. The location of the gathering will determine whether or not you'll be able to stand up and address the families and players (for example, at a restaurant, you might not be able to talk over the noise of the other customers).

It's important for you, as the coach, to recognize all of the players. Honor the ones who are aging out or moving to higher leagues. Look back on the season and talk about all of the progress that the team made. If you have any funny anecdotes, now's the time to share them and make everybody laugh. Thank the players for their time and effort and encourage them to continue playing and practicing, and if you're so inclined, invite them to play for you again.

95 | Recognize Each Player

Before the end-of-season get together, take some time to go through your notes and make sure that you have something to say about each player. You don't need to gush or overstate, but you want all of your players to leave knowing that you appreciate their individual contributions to the team. Make them feel as if they took part in making the team succeed by thanking them for their work, their attention at practice, and their willingness to work as a team. If you have the time and space, call the players up individually and have them stand by you while you acknowledge them—this makes what you're saying more personal. If you've kept statistics throughout the season, you might share some of them with the guests. Make sure to pick out the important ones that show the players' progression throughout the season.

96 | Do an End-of-the-Season "Wrap Up"

If you're coaching a school team, there are probably uniforms that need to be laundered and returned. Make sure that all of them are in good condition and clean. Also, inspect all of your equipment and figure out what needs to be replaced before the next season begins. Sit down with your school's athletic director to review the season and thank him for his support. Also, ask the AD if there are any problems or complaints that you should be aware of. Discuss the next season and talk about any teams on your schedule that you'd like to drop or add. Be sure to let the AD know if you need equipment for the next season or if there are any problems with the court or field.

If you've been coaching a club or recreational team, you can sit with the athletics coordinator to review the season. The discussion points would be similar to those for the school AD. If there are local rules that you would like to modify, eliminate, or update, let the coordinator know. This is also a good time to discuss officiating. Were you pleased with the officials? Give any positive and negative feedback to the coordinator—because he doesn't get to see every official in action, he might not be aware of which ones are good and which ones need improvement. If you were pleased with the officials, be sure to mention that.

97 | Thank Everyone

Throughout the season, take fifteen-to-twenty seconds after games to thank everyone who assisted. You don't have to do this at every game, but make sure to regularly express your gratitude. Thank the parents often for bringing their kids to practices and games on time.

If you do have an end-of-season celebration, the first person you should thank is your significant other, if applicable. Without his or her support and encouragement, your coaching career never would have gotten off the ground. Be sure to also thank the assistant coach, team parent, and all of the score keepers, stat takers, line judges, and snack bringers. You'll probably discover that the slightest bit of warmth and sincerity will make people much more inclined to help you out in the future.

98 | Ask for Feedback

You've given feedback, and now is the time to ask for some. This can be a humbling and sometimes frustrating experience. Some parents will be reluctant to say anything for fear that their input could affect their child's playing time. Others may hesitate for fear that their feedback will be construed as negative or confrontational. Be persistent—once the parents realize that you actually *want* feedback, they'll open up and help. This input is an excellent resource for figuring out what to work on either during this season or the next season. (Remember that it's only "constructive" criticism if you do something with it.)

Try to talk to the parents individually. Catch them at the start of practice or take a minute to sit in the bleachers with them if they're observing a practice. Lead the discussion by asking specific, open-ended questions, and let them know that if they'd like to think about it and get back to you, that's fine. Some good questions to ask are:

- What things can I do to improve the practices?
- What drills do you recommend?
- How can I improve as a coach?

Make sure to talk to all of the parents, follow up with them, and assure them that you think that their opinions are important. The second half of the season is a good time to start these discussions.

99 | Take Time to Evaluate Your Season as a Coach

The season is coming to a close. Time has flown by and the players have all developed new skills and improved upon old ones. You've gathered about all of the information possible from players, parents, and coordinators, and now is a good time to sit down and assess yourself as a coach.

This doesn't need to be a long, drawn-out process. Use the information that you received and sit down and take some notes. Begin the assessment at tryouts. Ask yourself, are there other ways of holding tryouts that you'd like to try? Were you satisfied with your initial assessments of the players' skills? Now think about practices. How can you pack more touches into the limited time? How could you use the assistant coach more effectively? Consider game day. Did you maximize players' time on the court or field? Were you satisfied with your substitution lists and patterns? Taking the time to think about your coaching techniques and working to discover opportunities for improvement will ensure that you'll be ready for the next season.

100 | Continuing Education

In business, you must constantly stay on top of your field, and the same goes for coaching. With the internet, there's no reason not to continue to read, explore, and learn more about the sport(s) you're coaching. Ultimately, only you can determine the value of what you read; there's a lot of junk on the web that's of little value, but finding a helpful site will fire you up and get you ready for the next season.

On the web, there's a variety of sites that will send you periodic notices about new drills, conditioning, and all of the other fine points of coaching (have a look at the appendix for some helpful sites). There are also a lot of helpful books out there, including the *For Dummies* series. If you become obsessed with coaching and really want to improve, check college sports websites, as many college coaches offer coaching clinics. National coaching organizations such as USA Volleyball offer coaching accreditation programs. Keep in mind that both of these options will cost you money and a weekend. The upside of this is that you'll get to meet lots of other coaches in an environment that encourages the exchange of ideas. Not only will you learn a great deal, but you will also make contacts and establish invaluable friendships.

101 | Let's Do it Again

Congratulations! You've made it through the season. I hope that you've enjoyed the journey and witnessed your players grow both individually and as a team. I also hope that you learned a few things in the process as well. If nothing else, you now have memories that will last long after the frustrations and impatience have been forgotten. Each of your coaching opportunities will be different; enjoy each team and try to learn at least one new thing, such as a drill, a play, a formation, a cheer, or a joke. All of these things will help you become a better coach.

Thank you for reading.

Appendix

Coaching Philosophy

This is an evolving philosophy that I've been working on for several years. I strive to challenge my players and encourage both their mental and physical growth as student athletes. The strong practice ethic, mental focus, and good sportsmanship learned on the court are applicable throughout the players' lives. I strive to provide a safe environment and competitive playing time for all student athletes. My philosophy on the volleyball court is based on four pillars.

The first pillar is that every player should develop a strong mental foundation. Every player will understand and execute solid form and technique, both offensively and defensively.

Second, a team can only succeed by working as a team. Each player will understand her position and where she needs to be.

Thirdly, open communication is essential. Every player will be heard, both on and off the court.

Finally, players must be focused at practice. Players need to execute in practice in the way that they would during a game, because what players do in practice will surface during games.

I don't expect my players to have a perfect focus all the time, but I will tell them when they need to bear down and concentrate. As a coach, I always come to practice well-prepared and with an objective in mind and a plan to accomplish it.

Coaching Objective

My objective for coaching is for my players, by the end of the season, to be able to say that they had fun playing volleyball on my team, that they improved their fundamental skills, and that they feel prepared to play at the next level of volleyball.

Coaching Websites

- winningvolleyballskills.com
- usavolleyball.org
- coachpatanderson.com

More Titles in the LifeTips Book Series

101 MORTGAGES TIPS
by Bill Pirraglia

101 SUCCESSFUL PR CAMPAIGN TIPS
by Mary White

101 ENGLISH GARDEN TIPS
by Sheri Ann Richerson

101 NATURAL HEALTHY EATING TIPS
by Emily Davidson

101 AUTHOR TIPS
by P.J. Campbell

Printed in the United States
153184LV00001B/15/P